Plants in Winter

BY JENNA LEE GLEISNER

The Child's World®
childsworld.com

Published by The Child's World®
1980 Lookout Drive • Mankato, MN 56003-1705
800-599-READ • www.childsworld.com

Photographs ©: Volodymyr Plysiuk/Shutterstock Images,
cover, 1; iStockphoto, 5, 8, 10–11; Shutterstock Images,
7, 12; Karen Bailey/Shutterstock Images, 15; Tony
Campbell/Shutterstock Images, 16–17; Leni Kovaleva/
Shutterstock Images, 18; Janno Loide/Shutterstock
Images, 21; Red Line Editorial, 22

ISBN 9781503823884
LCCN 2017944878

Printed in the United States of America
PA02359

ABOUT THE AUTHOR

Jenna Lee Gleisner is an author
and editor who lives in Minnesota.
She has written more than 80
books for children. When not
writing or editing, she enjoys
spending time with her family
and her dog, Norrie.

Contents

CHAPTER 1

Winter Cold...4

CHAPTER 2

Dormant...10

CHAPTER 3

Winter Plants...14

Evergreen Tree Craft...22
Glossary...23
To Learn More...24
Index...24

Winter Cold

It is winter. Winter comes after fall. Many trees lose their leaves.

Water freezes in winter. Ice forms on **bare** branches.

Winter is cold. Snow covers the ground.

Dormant

Most plants need warmth. They also need sunlight.

To **survive** winter,
plants stop growing.
They go **dormant**.

Winter Plants

Evergreen trees stay green. They keep their needles.

Birds make their homes in evergreen trees. The trees keep them warm.

Birch trees also survive in winter. These trees have white or silver **bark**.

Spring comes after winter.
Spring is warmer. Plants
will **sprout** again in spring.

Evergreen Tree Craft

Make your own evergreen tree!

Supplies:

black marker   paintbrush
paper   dried green herbs
glue   brown marker

Instructions:

1. Using the black marker, draw the outline of an evergreen tree onto the paper.

2. Use the paintbrush to spread glue on the inside of the tree.

3. Sprinkle the dried herbs onto the glue.

4. Using the brown marker, color the trunk of your evergreen tree.

Glossary

bare—(BAYR) Something that is bare is not covered. Many tree branches are bare in winter.

bark—(BARK) Bark is a rough covering on the outside of a tree. Birch trees have silver or white bark.

dormant—(DOR-muhnt) Dormant means alive but not growing. Many plants are dormant in winter.

sprout—(SPROWT) To sprout means to grow or appear. Leaves and plants will sprout again in spring.

survive—(sur-VYVE) To survive is to live through harsh conditions. Plants stop growing in winter to survive.

To Learn More

Books

Carr, Aaron. *Winter*. New York, NY: AV2 by Weigl, 2017.

Herrington, Lisa M. *How Do You Know It's Winter?* New York, NY: Children's Press, 2014.

Web Sites

Visit our Web site for links about plants in winter:

childsworld.com/links

Note to Parents, Teachers, and Librarians: We routinely verify our Web links to make sure they are safe and active sites. So encourage your readers to check them out!

Index

birch trees, 19

evergreen trees, 14, 16

ice, 6

leaves, 4

winter, 4, 6, 9, 13, 19, 20

24